ENDANGERED MOUNTAIN GORILLAS

Bobbie Kalman & Kristina Lundblad

Crabtree Publishing Company

www.crabtreebooks.com

Earth's Endangered Animals Series
A Bobbie Kalman Book

Dedicated by Kristina Lundblad
For my mom and dad, with love

Editor-in-Chief
Bobbie Kalman

Writing team
Bobbie Kalman
Kristina Lundblad

Editors
Molly Aloian
Amanda Bishop
Kelley MacAulay
Kathryn Smithyman

Art director
Robert MacGregor

Design
Katherine Kantor

Production Coordinator
Katherine Kantor

Photo research
Crystal Foxton

Consultant
Patricia Loesche, Ph.D., Animal Behavior Program,
Department of Psychology, University of Washington

Photographs
Joe McDonald: page 30
Minden Pictures: Konrad Wothe: pages 15 (bottom),
    17, 20, 22;
    Gerry Ellis: pages 24, 25, 28
Bruce Davidson/naturepl.com: page 10
Michael Leach/NHPA: page 26
© Fritz Polking/Visuals Unlimited: page 13
© Wolfgang Kaehler, www.wkaehlerphoto.com: page 27
Other images by Digital Stock and Digital Vision

Illustrations
All illustrations by Barbara Bedell

Crabtree Publishing Company

www.crabtreebooks.com   1-800-387-7650

Copyright © **2005 CRABTREE PUBLISHING COMPANY.**
All rights reserved. No part of this publication may be
reproduced, stored in a retrieval system or be transmitted in
any form or by any means, electronic, mechanical, photocopying,
recording, or otherwise, without the prior written permission
of Crabtree Publishing Company. In Canada: We acknowledge the
financial support of the Government of Canada through the Book
Publishing Industry Development Program (BPIDP) for our
publishing activities.

Cataloging-in-Publication Data
Kalman, Bobbie.
  Endangered mountain gorillas / Bobbie Kalman & Kristina
Lundblad.
    p. cm. -- (Earth's endangered animals series)
  Includes index.
  ISBN 0-7787-1855-7 (RLB) -- ISBN 0-7787-1901-4 (pbk.)
  1. Gorilla--Juvenile literature. 2. Endangered species--Juvenile
literature. I. Lundblad, Kristina. II. Title.
  QL737.P96K254 2004
  599.884--dc22
                                                    2004011480
                                                    LC

**Published in
the United States**
PMB16A
350 Fifth Ave.
Suite 3308
New York, NY
10118

**Published
in Canada**
616 Welland Ave.,
St. Catharines, Ontario,
Canada
L2M 5V6

**Published in the
United Kingdom**
73 Lime Walk
Headington
Oxford
OX3 7AD
United Kingdom

**Published
in Australia**
386 Mt. Alexander Rd.,
Ascot Vale (Melbourne)
VIC 3032

Contents

Endangered!

Mountain gorillas are **endangered**. Endangered animals are at risk of disappearing from the Earth forever. In the past, thousands of mountain gorillas lived in the **wild**, or natural places where animals live. Today, fewer than 380 mountain gorillas remain in the wild.

Animals in trouble

There are more than 1,000 known **species**, or types, of endangered animals on Earth today. In a few years, many of these species may become **extinct**. Mountain gorillas are very close to becoming extinct. Keep reading to learn more about mountain gorillas, why they are endangered, and how people can help them.

Words to know

Scientists use special words to describe animals in danger. Some of these words are listed below.

vulnerable Describes animals that may soon become endangered

endangered Describes animals that are in danger of disappearing from the Earth forever

critically endangered Describes animals that are at high risk of dying out in the wild

extinct Describes animals that have died out or have not been seen in the wild for at least 50 years

5

What are mountain gorillas?

Mountain gorillas are large animals, but they are peaceful and gentle. They rarely fight with one another or with other animals.

Mountain gorillas are **mammals**. All mammals are **warm-blooded** animals. The bodies of warm-blooded animals stay about the same temperature, no matter how warm or cold their surroundings are. Mammals have backbones, and most have hair or fur on their bodies. Baby mammals drink milk from their mothers' bodies.

Primates

Mountain gorillas belong to a group of mammals called **primates**. There are over 250 primate species, including monkeys, lemurs, great apes, and humans. Primates are intelligent animals. Mountain gorillas are **great apes**. Great apes are the largest primates. All great apes are endangered.

Five kinds of gorillas

Mountain gorillas are one of five **subspecies**, or kinds, of gorillas. These subspecies are split into two groups—eastern and western. The eastern lowland gorilla, the **Bwindi gorilla**, and the mountain gorilla belong to the eastern group. The western lowland gorilla and the Cross River gorilla belong to the western group. All gorillas live in different parts of Africa. Although they may live far from one another, they all face similar threats.

The western lowland gorilla lives in the tropical rain forests of west Africa.

Gorillas in danger

The eastern lowland gorilla and the western lowland gorilla (shown left) are both endangered. The mountain gorilla, the Cross River gorilla, and the Bwindi gorilla are critically endangered. Scientists try to **estimate** the total number of wild gorillas. It is difficult to know exactly how many mountain gorillas live in the wild because they do not live near people.

Gorilla homes

A **habitat** is the natural place where an animal lives. The mountain gorilla's habitat is the cool, misty forests that cover the Virunga Volcanoes. The Virunga Volcanoes are eight volcanoes that are surrounded by mountains. They are located in the central part of Africa, along the borders of Rwanda, Uganda, and the Democratic Republic of the Congo. The highest volcano is 14,787 feet (4507 m). Most mountain gorillas live high in the mountains—above 11,500 feet (3505 m)! Other animals that live in the Virunga Volcano forests include antelope, golden monkeys, and forest buffalo.

A mountain gorilla's body

Mountain gorillas have brownish-black hair all over their bodies, except on their faces, chests, the palms of their hands, and the soles of their feet.

Mountain gorillas have longer hair than other gorillas have. The long hair keeps these gorillas warm on the cool, high mountains where they live.

Mountain gorillas have powerful bodies. Male mountain gorillas are about twice as big as female mountain gorillas are. Each male weighs about 400 pounds (181 kg), whereas a female weighs about 200 pounds (91 kg).

Walking on all fours

A mountain gorilla's body is perfectly suited to moving around in the mountains. A mountain gorilla measures about six feet (1.8 m) in height when it stands up on its legs. It walks on all four **limbs**, supporting its weight on the knuckles of its hands. This way of walking is called **knuckle-walking**. Mountain gorillas can **trot**, but they prefer to travel slowly.

An older male mountain gorilla develops a crown of bone, muscle, and hair that makes his head look longer than a female's head.

A mountain gorilla's legs are shorter than its arms are.

A mountain gorilla has five fingers on each hand and five toes on each foot.

Hanging on

Like all primates, mountain gorillas have hands with four fingers and one thumb. Each finger and thumb has a fingernail and a fingerprint. A mountain gorilla's hand is **prehensile**, or able to grasp. A mountain gorilla can use its hands to pick up objects or hold onto branches.

A mountain gorilla's life cycle

Like all living things, a mountain gorilla goes through a set of **stages**, or changes, in its life called a **life cycle**. A mountain gorilla's life cycle begins inside its mother's body. A baby gorilla develops and grows for eight to nine months, until it is ready to be born.

A female mountain gorilla usually has only one baby at a time, but sometimes a female has twins. A young mountain gorilla is called a **juvenile** until it becomes **mature**, or adult. Mature mountain gorillas are able to **mate**, or join together to make babies.

A male mountain gorilla is mature at eleven to thirteen years of age. A female mountain gorilla matures between the ages of ten and twelve.

A newborn mountain gorilla weighs about four to five pounds (1.8-2.3 kg).

Juvenile mountain gorillas are very playful! They climb trees, roll around on the ground, chase one another, and wrestle.

*A baby mountain gorilla **nurses**, or drinks its mother's milk, for about one year. It then starts eating other foods as well. It stops nursing completely at three to four years of age.*

12

Growing up

A baby mountain gorilla grows quickly. At three to four months, it can sit upright and crawl. Soon afterward, it is able to stand. The baby can grip tightly with its hands. It uses its grip to cling to the hairs on its mother's stomach. When the baby is a little older and stronger, it rides on its mother's back. A juvenile stays with its mother for three to four years after it is born. It then lives apart from its mother but remains in the same family group (see pages 14-15).

Forming a new group

A male gorilla leaves his group when he is about eleven years old. He lives alone until he finds a female partner. The male and female mountain gorillas then mate and form a new family group.

*An animal's **life span** is the length of time it is alive. Mountain gorillas usually live between 40 and 50 years.*

Family groups

Mountain gorillas live in groups that include several family members. Some groups have only two members, whereas others have over 30. A typical group has five to ten members. The mountain gorillas in each group care for and protect one another. Most groups include one **silverback**. A silverback is a mature male whose fur has turned silvery gray over time. Young adult males are called **blackbacks** because the color of their fur has not yet changed.

Groups often include one or two younger males, a few females, and some juveniles and babies.

The group leader

The leader of a mountain gorilla group is the biggest and strongest mature male. He is almost always a silverback. A group may have more than one silverback, but only one silverback is **dominant** in the group.

In charge!

The dominant silverback is in charge of the group's daily travels in search of food. He also decides when and where the group will rest. The dominant silverback is the father of most of the babies in the group.

Silverbacks are gentle and playful with the young mountain gorillas in their family groups. They allow babies to tug on their hair and ride on their backs.

A silverback stops other mountain gorillas from fighting and protects the group from danger.

15

Mountain gorilla behavior

Eating and sleeping

Mountain gorillas spend much of the day eating. At night, they build nests for sleeping. Small, light mountain gorillas may nest in trees, but heavy gorillas make grass nests on the ground. Babies and mothers snuggle in the same nests.

Keeping clean

To stay healthy, mountain gorillas must keep very clean. Mountain gorillas **groom**, or clean, one another. They clean dirt and bugs out of one another's fur with their lips and fingers. Female mountain gorillas groom their babies.

16

Gorilla talk

Mountain gorillas **communicate**, or send messages to one another, using facial expressions, sounds, and **gestures**. After eating, they make soft purring and grunting sounds to show that they have had enough to eat.

Angry sounds

To show anger, mountain gorillas open their mouths and show their teeth. Silverbacks make hooting sounds to keep their groups close together. Females grunt when they scold their young.

*When threatened by an attacker, a group's silverback stands on his legs, pounds on his chest, shows his teeth, and pretends to **charge**. This behavior is meant to frighten the attacker, not harm him.*

Food in the forest

Mountain gorillas spend many hours each day looking for food and eating. They are **herbivores**, or animals that eat mainly plants. They feed in open, sunny parts of the forests where many plants grow.

Mountain gorillas eat different types and parts of plants, such as leaves, flowers, fruits, bamboo shoots, and roots. They do not need to drink much water. They get enough water from the plants they eat.

Finding food

To get food from trees, mountain gorillas shake fruit off high branches or pick fruit from the low branches. Some group members climb trees to reach certain foods, but mountain gorillas are not good climbers. Once a mountain gorilla has climbed up a tree, it may take the gorilla a long time to get back down!

An adult male gorilla can eat up to 50 pounds (23 kg) of plant food in one day!

Habitat loss

The biggest threat to mountain gorillas is **habitat loss**. Habitat loss means losing the areas in which animals live and find food. People cause habitat loss by **clearing**, or removing the trees from, forests to create farmland. There are more people on Earth each year, and they need more room and food. People plant crops where trees and plants once grew. They also raise cattle in the areas that they have cleared. Mountain gorillas now compete with both cattle and people for food.

*By taking over the land, people also **pollute** the homes of mountain gorillas. They litter the land with garbage and make a lot of noise. Noise disturbs gorillas.*

Trouble in the forest

People have also taken over mountain gorilla habitats to escape war. In 1994, a war in Rwanda forced many people to leave their homes and live in the forests. To survive, some people had to hunt mountain gorillas for food. They also sold mountain gorilla body parts to make money. Today, the fighting continues in some parts of Rwanda, Uganda, and the Democratic Republic of the Congo. Mountain gorilla habitats are threatened in all these countries.

When local people build new roads in the forests, it is easier for hunters to find the mountain gorillas living there.

21

Fewer mountain gorillas

*Mountain gorillas have few natural **predators**. They are sometimes killed by leopards, but their greatest predators by far are humans.*

The mountain gorilla **population** is very low. Population is the total number of one kind of animal. One reason for the low mountain gorilla population is that these animals have few babies. Male and female mountain gorillas are not able to mate until they are over ten years old. A female then has only one baby every three to four years.

Not getting older

Even when a baby mountain gorilla is born, it may not grow to be an adult. Many young gorillas are hunted or die from illnesses before they are able to have their own babies. When young gorillas are killed, even fewer animals reach ten or more years of age. The population then drops even more because the animals that were killed never mature and have babies.

Hunting gorillas

Poachers are people who hunt and kill animals illegally. Some poachers kill mountain gorillas and sell their body parts. Poachers also set traps for other animals that live in the mountains, such as antelope and bush pigs. Mountain gorillas sometimes get caught in these traps.

Stealing babies

Some poachers also steal mountain gorilla babies and sell them as pets. Female mountain gorillas are very protective of their babies, so poachers often kill the mother in order to steal the baby. Sometimes poachers kill an entire group of mountain gorillas just to take one baby!

Safe places

Many people are working hard to protect mountain gorillas. The parts of gorilla habitats that have not been destroyed are now protected as **national parks**. In these parks, mountain gorillas are free to roam, eat, and nest. The trees and plants they need for food and shelter grow right where the gorillas live. Other kinds of animals live in the parks as well and are also protected.

Although many gorillas live in zoos, there are no mountain gorillas in captivity. Zookeepers do not accept mountain gorillas because they are so endangered. The gorillas at zoos are usually western or eastern lowland gorillas.

24

Keeping a close watch

Scientists and **park rangers** patrol the parks daily. They keep track of the mountain gorillas and other animals. They help the sick or injured animals. Park rangers also try to keep mountain gorillas and other animals safe from poachers. They remove any traps that poachers have set. During times of war, park rangers, such as the one above, risk their lives to protect mountain gorillas!

Visiting mountain gorillas

Many people are very interested in mountain gorillas. People from all over the world travel to Africa just to see these animals up-close. Visiting and observing natural areas and animals is called **ecotourism**. **Tourists**, or people who like to travel, pay about $250 US each to spend just one hour with the gorillas! The money is used to protect mountain gorillas and the forests in which they live. Tourists also spend a lot of money on hotels and restaurants in the areas they visit. Uganda, Rwanda, and the Democratic Republic of the Congo make millions of dollars each year from ecotourism. This money supports local people and businesses.

Dangerous diseases

People who visit mountain gorillas must be careful not to make the gorillas sick. Mountain gorillas can catch diseases, such as **pneumonia**, from humans. Diseases are dangerous for mountain gorillas. If one mountain gorilla becomes ill, other members of the group can also become ill. Even a disease that is fairly harmless to humans can destroy an entire gorilla population. Tourists are taken through the forests by tour guides to make sure they do not get too close to the animals. Tourists are required to get **vaccines** before they visit the areas in which the gorillas live.

People must follow strict rules when they visit mountain gorillas. Trained tour guides make sure that the visitors do not disturb the animals.

People helping gorillas

People help mountain gorillas in special ways. Some scientists study these animals in the wild. They learn what mountain gorillas eat and what they need to survive. They also study their behavior. Other people work hard to pass laws that punish poachers and the people who buy the animal parts that the poachers sell. Many of the people who live near the forests of the Virunga Volcanoes are poor farmers. They need to grow food to survive. One way scientists help mountain gorillas is by working with these local people. They teach them how to grow food without cutting down more areas of the forest.

Making a difference

The **Dian Fossey Gorilla Fund International** is an organization that works hard to protect mountain gorillas. Dian Fossey researched mountain gorillas for 22 years while living with them in Africa. She also started a research center in Rwanda called the Karisoke Research Center. Today, the Dian Fossey Gorilla Fund International continues to study mountain gorillas and works hard to find better ways to protect them.

Great gorilla news!

Helping mountain gorillas works! Mountain gorillas are still in danger, but the many people who study and protect them are making a difference. In 1989, scientists estimated that there were 324 mountain gorillas living in the wild. In 2003, the gorillas were counted again. Scientists estimated that there were 380 mountain gorillas, living in 30 separate family groups. Keep reading to find out how you, too, can help save mountain gorillas!

Amazing apes!

Mountain gorillas may live far away, but you can still help them! Learn all you can about these amazing apes and share what you know with others. For example, did you know that young mountain gorillas lose their teeth just like children do? When young mountain gorillas are five to six years of age, they start losing their baby teeth. New teeth grow in to replace the teeth they have lost. Share this fun fact and more with your friends at school by writing a story about a mountain gorilla family. You can even paint pictures of mountain gorillas in their forest homes to go with your story!

Start surfing!

Learn all about mountain gorillas and other endangered animals by checking out these websites:

• **www.nationalgeographic.com/kids**—Click on "Creature Features" and then click on mountain gorillas

• **www.worldwildlifefund.org/gorillas/index.cfm**

• **www.gorillafund.org**—Learn about The Dian Fossey Gorilla Fund International

By saving the habitats of mountain gorillas, people are also saving thousands of other plants and animals that live in the same area!

Glossary

Note: Boldfaced words that are defined in the text may not appear in the glossary.

Bwindi gorilla A gorilla subspecies that lives in Uganda's Bwindi Impenetrable National Park and does not yet have a scientific name

captivity A state of being in an enclosed area such as a zoo

charge To attack by rushing forward

dominant Describing an animal that is in charge of other animals or has the most control

estimate To count approximately, not exactly

gesture A hand or body movement used for communication

limb A body part such as a leg, arm, or wing

national park An area of land set aside by a country to protect the plants and animals that live within it

pneumonia A disease caused by a virus in which the lungs become inflamed and fill with fluid

pollute To add harmful waste, making an area unfit for living things

predator An animal that hunts and kills other animals for food

trot To move quickly

vaccine A substance that is swallowed or injected into the body that helps protect the body from a certain disease

Index

1 2 3 4 5 6 7 8 9 0 Printed in the U.S.A. 4 3 2 1 0 9 8 7 6 5